Are dragons real?

Contents

Written by Isabel Thomas

Collins

1 Here be dragons

Close your eyes and imagine a dragon.

How many of these features does your dragon have?

Even though we haven't seen a dragon in real life, we know what they look like!

fiery breath

wings

sharp teeth

scales

fearsome claws

four legs

large nostrils

sticking-up ears

horns or spikes

eyes like a lizard

long tail

2

People have been telling stories about dragons for a long time. The dragons that we see in books, films and TV shows are based on old stories about dragons.

But where did those old stories come from?

Have you heard the saying: "Here be dragons"?

It's an old-fashioned way to say, "Dragons live here". It was first written on a map that is 500 years old.

On this map, the words "Here be dragons" are written in an **ancient** language called Latin.

This map was one of the very first **globes** ever made in Europe. The person who made it was trying to show facts about the world.

Other old maps also include pictures of dragons.

Does this mean that dragons were once animals that could be seen in real life, and not just in stories? To find out, we need to go back in time and look at the very first stories about dragons. We need to ask questions:

- How did these stories begin?
- Is there any **evidence** that dragons once existed?
- Is there any evidence that they still do?

2 Dragons in stories

Myths and legends are stories that have been told for a very long time. They are told as if they really happened, but they are **unproven**.

Dragons appear in myths and legends from many different times and places.

In one Ancient Greek myth, a hero called Jason goes on a quest to find a golden fleece. A dragon guards the fleece.

Greek myths also tell of a king who grew new armies by planting dragon teeth in the soil, instead of seeds!

The word dragon comes from the Ancient Greek word *drakon*. It means monster with eyes that watch, or monster with evil eyes.

What is the difference between myths and legends?

▶ Myths are well-known stories that often feature magical creatures or events. People know that myths are not true, but they carry important messages.

▶ Legends are stories that some people think may be based on facts. But no one has yet **proven** they are true.

7

Dragons also star in Ancient Chinese myths and legends. These stories tell of dragons that are powerful, but not as fierce as the dragons in Ancient Greek myths.

Dragons were said to puff out storm clouds, bringing rain.

Instead, they have the power to control the weather, water and seasons. They may even be kind and helpful, and bring good luck. In these stories, the dragons are the heroes!

Dragon stories from Ancient China are the oldest in the world. We know about them from books and art made at the time.

This jade dragon was carved around 6,000 years ago. It has a long snout and narrow eyes.

Longan or "dragon eye" trees are named after the Chinese word for dragon – *long*. When you peel the fruits, they look a bit like dragon eyeballs!

In the **Middle Ages**, dragon **folktales** became very popular in Europe. The dragons were not helpful and lucky like the dragons in East Asian mythology. They were dangerous and mean!

In some stories, they hid in caves, guarding treasure!

They were said to breathe fire!

They feasted on sheep – or even people!

People, not dragons, are the heroes of these stories. In many stories, the dragon is eventually **slain** by a brave person. A famous one is the legend of St George and the Dragon. It has been retold in different ways for more than 900 years.

In this famous story, George kills a dragon to stop it from eating a princess.

Almost every part of the world has its own **traditional** stories about dragons.

Every dragon is different. Some have wings and breathe fire. Some have more than one head. Some are small, while others are giant. Some live in the sea, while others hide in caves and mountains.

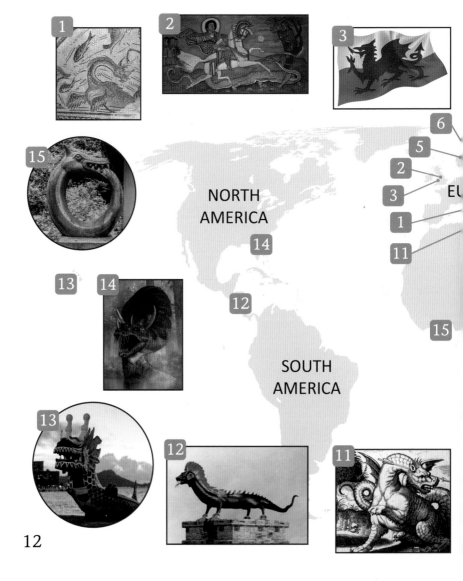

But these dragons also have lots in common, such as snake-like bodies, scales and claws.

Why did so many different people, from so many different times and places, come up with such similar stories?

Is it possible that these myths and legends were based on real animals?

ASIA

OCEANIA

3 Fact or fiction?

How do you tell if something is real, or just a story? If it is fact or **fiction**?

Seeing something with your own eyes is the best way to tell if something is real. Scientists and **historians** do this. Instead of just believing what they are told, they ask for evidence.

I saw a photograph.

I saw it with my own eyes.

I saw it on the news.

But what if it's impossible to see something with your own eyes? For example, we can't see animals that lived long ago, because they are now **extinct**.

So, scientists and historians look for other kinds of evidence, such as:

- measurements made by machines
- eyewitness accounts
- artefacts
- **fossils**.

Then, they work out how **reliable** this evidence is!

I heard about it from someone else.

I saw it in a book.

Is there any evidence that dragons are real? And can we trust it?

There are clues in ancient books. Almost 2,000 years ago, an author called Philostratus wrote about different types of dragons that were said to live in India.

In the same book, Philostratus wrote about real animals, such as elephants, sharks and whales. He thought dragons were real too.

However, Philostratus did not travel to India himself. He was writing about someone else's adventures. This makes it harder to trust his description of dragons.

a description of dragons by Philostratus

The dragons of
the mountains
have scales of
a golden colour,
and in length **excel**
those of the plain,
and they have
bushy beards, which also are of a golden **hue**;
and their eye is sunk deep under the eyebrow,
and **emits** a terrible and ruthless **glance**.
And they give off a noise like the clashing of
brass whenever they are burrowing under
the earth, and from their crests, which are
all fiery red, there flashes a fire brighter
than a torch.

Just over 1,500 years ago, an Ancient Chinese book gave instructions about how to turn dragon bones into medicine.

"For using dragon's bones, first cook odorous plants; bathe the bones twice in hot water, pound them to powder ..."

18

It is likely that people really did use ground-up bones as medicine. The same book contains lots of traditional treatments that are still used today.

However, there is no evidence that these bones were really dragon bones. Powdered "dragon bones" and "dragon tooth" are still used in traditional Chinese medicine to treat some illnesses. But they are ground-up fossils.

In the Middle Ages, people began trying to record the history of England in a huge book called the *Anglo-Saxon Chronicle*.

Every year, for hundreds of years, people recorded the things that happened. In 793 CE, they recorded a dragon sighting in the north of England!

> "*Here were dreadful forewarnings come over the land of Northumbria, and* **woefully** *terrified the people: these were amazing sheets of lightning and whirlwinds, and fiery dragons were seen flying in the sky.*"

Historians think the *Anglo-Saxon Chronicle* is the best **source** of evidence for the history of England at that time.

Today, we think the "fiery dragons" may have been a **meteor** shower. Before people knew about the science of space, they may have explained shooting stars by comparing them to things they *had* heard about – such as dragons!

21

In the Middle Ages, many old books were rewritten in other languages.

One of these was an ancient science book called *Natural History*, written by a famous Roman author called Pliny.

In this book, Pliny wrote about dragons alongside real animals, such as elephants and lions. He said that elephants and dragons were always fighting and he described these fights in detail.

We know that Pliny wrote his book very carefully. He listed his sources. He described many mammals, reptiles, fish, birds and insects that are real.

But most of Pliny's sources were even older books. He didn't see these animals with his own eyes.

Might the elephants have been fighting a completely different animal?

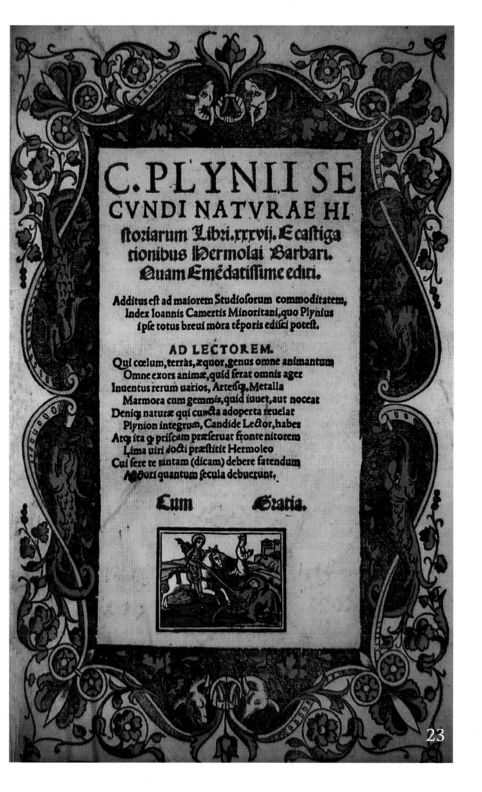

C.PLYNII SE
CVNDI NATVRAE HI
ſtoriarum Libri.xxxvij. E caſtiga
tionibus Hermolai Barbari.
Quam Emédatiſſime editi.

Additus eſt ad maiorem Studioſorum commoditatem,
Index Ioannis Camertis Minoritani,quo Plynius
ipſe totus breui mora téporis ediſci poteſt.

AD LECTOREM.

Qui cœlum,terràs,æquor,genus omne animantum
  Omne exors animæ,quid ſerat omnis ager
Inuentus rerum uarios, Arteſqʒ,Metalla
  Marmora cum gemmis,quid iuuet,aut noceat
Deniqʒ naturæ qui cuncta adoperta reuelat
  Plynion integrum, Candide Lector,habes
Atqʒ ita qʒ priſcam præſeruat fronte nitorem
  Lima uiri docti præſtitit Hermoleo
Cui ſere te tantam (dicam) debere ſatendum
  Authori quantum ſecula debuerunt.

Cum   Gratia.

4 Dragonlike animals

What kinds of real animals might have inspired stories about dragons?

There is a clue on the globe that says "Here be dragons". The words are written next to Southeast Asia. In the Middle Ages, Chinese sailors reported seeing dragons on islands in this area.

Today, we know that these islands – Komodo, Rinca, Padar and Flores – are home to the world's largest living lizards. Lizards so big they have been named Komodo dragons!

Although they only got this name 100 years ago, Komodo dragons have been living on Earth for 90 million years.

They are fierce hunters, with powerful jaws. They will try to eat almost any other animal, including other Komodo dragons!

In the Middle Ages, sightings of huge lizards in Southeast Asia would have made dragon stories sound more believable.

But what animals might have inspired dragon stories in other parts of the world?

A fully grown Komodo dragon can be as long as two cows!

Many reptiles share the features of dragons:

Pythons are some of the world's largest snakes. They wrap their long bodies around **prey** and squeeze it to death. Perhaps they inspired stories of dragons coiling their tails around elephants. Pythons were named after a dragon-serpent from Greek myths!

Chinese alligators are large reptiles that lurk in water. Perhaps they inspired the myths of water dragons in Ancient China.

Goannas or monitor lizards have sharp teeth and claws. They appear in traditional stories.

Nile crocodiles and saltwater crocodiles are the largest living reptiles. In the past, they may have swum across oceans to countries where they didn't normally live. Imagine seeing these huge reptiles on a beach. You might think it was a magical creature!

Many old drawings of dragons show snake-like bodies and very small legs, or no legs.

Birds are the close relatives of reptiles. Perhaps the wings and fearsome talons of dragons were inspired by birds of prey.

But all these animals are smaller than the dragons in old drawings. None of them breathes fire or has wings.

Perhaps it wasn't living animals that inspired dragon stories – but ancient animals!

eagle

Fossils help us learn about animals that lived long ago but are now extinct.

> Fossils are special rocks that formed
> millions of years ago, taking
> the shape of animals and plants
> that lived (and died) at that time.
> They show us how life on Earth has
> changed over time.

This is the fossil **skull** of a woolly rhinoceros.
These huge animals died out around 14,000 years ago.

Imagine digging up this skull thousands of years ago, before anyone knew about fossils or extinct animals. You might have imagined it was the head of a dragon!

This is exactly what happened in the town of Klagenfurt, Austria, in the Middle Ages. The people of the town kept the skull on display. They told a story about a snake-like dragon or *Lindwurm* that ate anyone who visited the local marshes. At the end of the story, the *Lindwurm* was slain by knights.

In the 1500s, they used the woolly rhinoceros's skull to design this sculpture of the *Lindwurm*.

There are other ancient fossils that may have inspired dragon stories. Most of them are fossils of extinct reptiles that were much larger than today's reptiles.

Titanoboa was a giant snake that lived 60 million years ago. It had a body as long as a bus (13 metres).

Megalania was the largest lizard that ever lived. This giant monitor lizard grew up to five metres long and weighed as much as a sea lion! It had curved teeth and sharp claws for tearing through prey.

Ichthyosaurs are nicknamed "sea dragons". They lived in water and had very large teeth and eyes.

But biggest of all extinct land animals were the dinosaurs!

Did dinosaur bones inspire dragon stories?

Can you see similarities between this Stegosaurus fossil and pictures of dragons?

Dinosaurs were first described and named by scientists around 200 years ago. Before this, no one knew these huge, extinct animals had once roamed Earth. But people had dug up the fossils of dinosaur bones, teeth, claws, spikes, and even scaly skin.

Just like today's scientists, they would have tried to imagine what the owner of these bones looked like. Sometimes, they were said to be dragon bones.

Dinosaur fossils are found all around the world. This could explain why dragons feature in traditional stories from so many different places.

Dracorex was a pachycephalosaur with spikes on its head. Its fossils are found in the "Badlands" of South Dakota, USA. Hundreds of years ago, it may have inspired traditional stories about a dragonlike water monster.

5 Are dragons possible?

New fossils of extinct animals are discovered all the time. Sometimes scientists even name them after dragons!

We know these are really dinosaurs and pterosaurs. But what if there are dragon fossils and we just haven't found them yet?

To answer this, let's take a closer look at the features of dragons in traditional stories and ask if they *could* be real.

This pterosaur was named Cryodrakon or "frozen dragon".

This sauropod was named the dragon of Qijiang.

Could an animal breathe fire?

No living animals can breathe fire. Reptiles are cold-blooded animals which means they can't make their own body heat. They have to move around or lie in the sun to warm up. Could a reptile really make enough heat to roast a sheep or singe a knight?

No living animals make fire, but there are animals that can make electricity, and animals that can release a jet of boiling liquid in self-defence!

We also know that animals warm up as they move their muscles (think about how warm you feel when you exercise). The larger an animal is, the more risk that it overheats. Perhaps a large dragon could become warm enough to spark fire!

But could such a large reptile ever fly?

Electric eels release a jolt of electricity to stun fish and make them easier to catch.

Bombardier beetles spray a jet of boiling liquid at predators.

Could a large reptile fly?

Birds are the only reptile relatives with wings. Most birds are very small and light. The largest birds can't fly.

But these large birds still have wings. Perhaps dragons had wings but couldn't fly. There are reptiles like this alive today.

Cassowaries have wings but can't fly.

Tiny Draco lizards have folds of skin that form "wings" when they fold their rib bones outwards. They can glide from tree to tree.

We also know that it's possible for very large animals to fly if they are light enough. Giant pterosaurs were reptile-like animals with leathery wings, made from huge folds of skin. Some were as small as today's birds. But the largest had a neck as long as a giraffe, with wings as wide as an Olympic running track!

However, look closely at a pterosaur and a dragon. Can you spot an important difference?

Could an animal have six limbs?

Dragons are said to have four legs and a pair of wings – a total of six **limbs**.

But pterosaurs (and every other animal with a backbone) have a maximum of four limbs!

These limbs might be formed into flippers, wings, arms or legs. They might be very tiny. But there are never more than four limbs altogether. Count them!

No animal with a backbone has ever had six limbs.
So, scientists think it is very unlikely that a dragon
with six limbs could have **evolved**.

6 Are dragons real?

We haven't found any reliable evidence that dragons are real. There are no dragon fossils.

But we have found evidence that traditional stories about dragons were based on real animals. These might have been living animals, including fierce reptiles such as huge snakes or Komodo dragons. Or they might have been extinct animals, known only by their bones and fossils.

Many features of dragons are found in these real animals. Perhaps human imaginations added the other features – such as fiery breath and six limbs!

Leonardo da Vinci was famous for his big imagination! He loved to imagine dragons, by combining features from different animals. Try it yourself!

"For a dragon, take the head of a dog, and give him the eyes of a cat, the ears of a porcupine, the nose of a greyhound, the eyebrows of a lion and the neck of a sea turtle."

Today we know that dragons are not likely to be real. But dragon stories are still popular all around the world.

Glossary

ancient thousands of years old, or older

emits sends out

evidence facts or information that support a belief or idea

evolved developed from other living things, but changed gradually, over time

excel being really good at something

extinct a living thing that once existed, but has died out

fiction a made-up story

folktales popular stories that have been told in a certain place for a long time; often passed on by word of mouth

fossils rocks that show us the shape of a plant or animal that lived long ago

glance a quick look

globes spherical maps of the world

historians people who study the past

hue a colour or shade

limbs arms, legs, wings or fins that stick out from an animal's body

meteor a space rock that is falling to Earth

Middle Ages a time in history from around 500 to 1500

prey an animal hunted for food

proven tried and tested

reliable can be trusted

skull the head bones of an animal

slain killed

source place where evidence comes from

traditional something that has been done in a certain way, for a long time

unproven has not been proven

woefully badly

Index

Here be dragons

4000 BCE

800 BCE

77 CE

500 CE

46

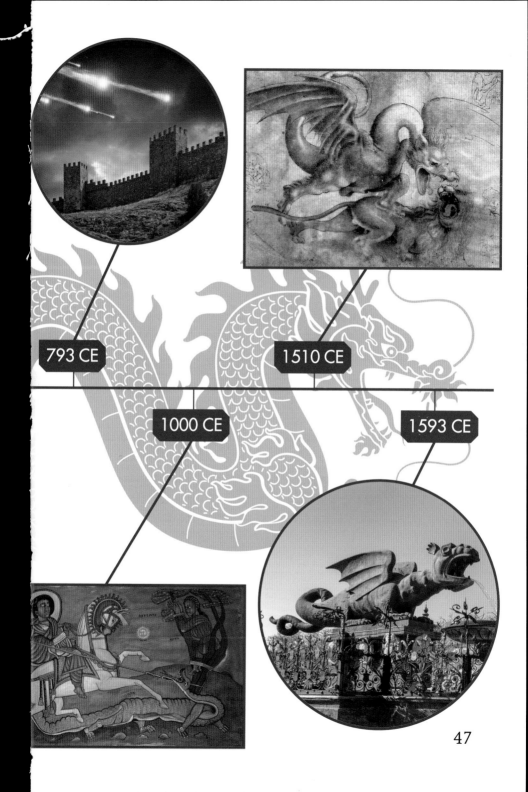

793 CE

1510 CE

1000 CE

1593 CE

Ideas for reading

Written by Christine Whitney
Primary Literacy Consultant

Reading objectives:
- be introduced to non-fiction books that are structured in different ways
- listen to, discuss and express views about non-fiction
- retrieve and record information from non-fiction
- discuss and clarify the meanings of words

Spoken language objectives:
- participate in discussion
- speculate, hypothesise, imagine and explore ideas through talk
- ask relevant questions

Curriculum links: History: Develop an awareness of the past; Writing: Write for different purposes

Word count: 3022

Interest words: evidence, historians, fiction, proven, unproven

Resources: paper, pencils and crayons

Build a context for reading

- Ask children to draw a dragon and to share their drawings with the group. What features have they drawn? Wings? Scales? Fire-breathing mouths?
- Ask children if they know of any stories or songs about dragons. Be prepared to direct them to a story or song for them to read or hear.
- Show the book cover to them and read the title, *Are dragons real?* Ask the group to consider the question and then take a vote and see if they believe that dragons are real or not.

Understand and apply reading strategies

- Read together up to the end of Chapter 1. Ask children to read the list of features on page 2 and check their drawings against this list. Are there any features listed there that are not on their drawings?
- Continue to read to the end of Chapter 2. Ask children to summarise how dragons are portrayed in different parts of the world.
- Read on to the end of Chapter 4. Challenge children to explain which *animals might have inspired dragon stories* in different parts of the world.